My Little Gol

ᴛʜᴇ SOLaR

By DENNIS R. SHEALY
Illustrated by RICHARD JOHNSON

The editors would like to thank Amie Gallagher, Planetarium Director,
Raritan Valley Community College, for her assistance
in the preparation of this book.

A GOLDEN BOOK • NEW YORK

Educators and librarians, for a variety of teaching tools, visit us at
RHTeachersLibrarians.com
Library of Congress Control Number: 2017943551
ISBN 978-1-5247-6684-9 (trade) — ISBN 978-1-5247-6685-6 (ebook)
Printed in the United States of America
10 9 8 7 6 5 4 3 2 1

Big Dipper

shooting star

Have you ever gazed into the night sky and wondered about all those twinkling lights? Maybe you've been lucky enough to see a shooting star! Or perhaps someone has shown you a *constellation*—a group of stars that forms a picture.

Most of those lights are very distant stars, but some of them are much closer. They are the planets that make up our Solar System.

Venus

Sun

Mercury

Earth

Mars

Jupiter

Saturn

Uranus

Neptune

At the center of our Solar System is the Sun. Like all stars, it's a ball of hot, glowing gases. It provides light and heat to Earth. Traveling around the Sun are Earth and seven other planets: Mercury, Venus, Mars, Jupiter, Saturn, Uranus, and Neptune. They receive light and heat from the Sun, too.

An *orbit* is the path one object takes around another object. Earth takes one year to travel around—or orbit—the Sun.

Neptune is the planet that is farthest from the Sun. It takes almost 165 years to orbit the Sun!

Mercury, the planet closest to the Sun, circles it the fastest—in just eighty-eight days!

Even though Mercury is closer to the Sun, Venus is the hottest planet. Gases in that planet's atmosphere trap the Sun's heat, making the average temperature there a sweltering 864 degrees!

Mercury

Venus

We can often see Venus easily on a clear night because it's so bright.

Our planet, Earth, is very special. As far as we know, it is the only planet in the universe with life! Earth has the kind of air, food, and water needed to support living things.

Earth rotates every twenty-four hours, what we call a day. During that time, half of Earth is turned toward the Sun, giving it light. The other half is dark. So while you're asleep, a child on the other side of the planet is awake and playing in the sunshine! At night, and sometimes in the daytime, we can see the one Moon that orbits Earth.

The Moon is a hunk of airless, waterless rock with craters and mountains. Its pale light, which is reflected from the Sun, has lit the way for humans at night for thousands of years.

The Moon is Earth's only natural satellite.
A *satellite* is an object that orbits a larger object.
Other planets have satellites, too.

There are also man-made satellites. Weather and
communication satellites, space stations, and space
telescopes all orbit our planet.

Mars is known as the Red Planet. It has lots of iron in its soil that has become like red rust. Powerful windstorms carry this dust all over the planet.

Scientists have sent many space probes to Mars. They have discovered that Mars once had water on its surface—which means it might also have had life! Perhaps one day humans will be able to land on this nearby planet.

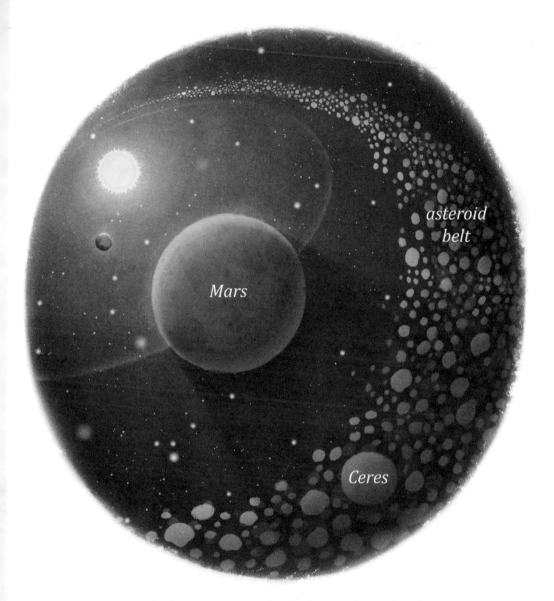

Beyond Mars is a vast belt that orbits the Sun.
The belt is made up of millions of space rocks called
asteroids. A few of them are very big. One asteroid
named Ceres is so big, it's called a *dwarf planet.*

The next four planets in our Solar
System are called *gas giants.* Unlike the
first four planets, which are mostly made
of solid rock, the gas giants are mostly
made of gases such as hydrogen and
helium. Jupiter is the largest gas giant
and the largest planet in the Solar System.
More than 1,300 Earths could fit inside it!
    Jupiter is famous for its big red "eye."
That eye is actually a giant windstorm—
like a hurricane on Earth—with winds
that blast over four hundred miles per
hour. The storm has been raging for
more than two hundred years! Jupiter
has fifty-three known moons, and may
have as many as sixty-seven.

Jupiter

All the gas giants have rings, but Saturn's rings are the brightest and the most famous. The rings look as if they're made of light, but they're actually made of rocks, dust, and ice racing around the planet at high speed.

Saturn

*rocks, dust,
and ice*

Saturn has more than sixty
moons. Scientists think the rings
may be made of material from
other moons that were shattered
by asteroids. That material
can be as small as a grain
of sand or as large as
a house!

Uranus

Unlike the other planets in the Solar System, Uranus is tilted almost completely sideways. Scientists think that a very large object may have smashed into it and knocked it over. Uranus gets its blue color from the methane gas in its atmosphere. It is almost an exact twin of the next and last planet in the Solar System: Neptune.

The beautiful blue planet Neptune takes 165 years to make one trip around the Sun, and its temperature is more than 350 degrees below zero! Similar to Jupiter, Neptune has a massive storm churning in its atmosphere. We call it the Dark Spot. This storm is the size of Earth!

Pluto was once considered the ninth planet, but due to its size—it's smaller than Earth's Moon—it has been reclassified as a dwarf planet. Another object named Eris was recently discovered in our Solar System, and it is about the same size as Pluto.

Pluto

We know about the Solar System because we have studied it with telescopes for hundreds of years. We have visited the Moon and actually walked on its surface. And we've sent robotic explorers to all the planets. Several rovers have rolled across the surface of Mars. The *Cassini* space probe orbited Saturn, its rings, and its moons for more than twelve years. The *New Horizons* spacecraft flew past Pluto.

We've also launched deep-space probes, such as *Voyager 1* and *Voyager 2*. They have been traveling far into space for more than forty years and are still sending information back to Earth.

From our little blue planet circling the Sun,
we are constantly discovering new things about
our Solar System. Perhaps we will one day live
on the Moon or Mars, or even travel to distant
solar systems in the Milky Way galaxy.

Where would YOU like to go?